EXIT SMART

VOL. 6

EXIT SMART

VOL. 6

Spotlights on Leading Exit Planning Advisors

LEADING EXIT PLANNING ADVISORS

FEATURING

Akili M. Johnson

Rick J. Krebs

Paul Moretti

Eric Cooper

Kelly Berenbaum

Linda A. Hamilton

Kyle Bochat

Kyle Danner

Rik Saylor

Exit Smart Vol. 6/ Mark Imperial —1st ed.

Chief Editor/ Shannon Buritz

ISBN: 978-1-954757-34-9

Remarkable Press™

Royalties from the retail sales of **"EXIT SMART Vol. 6: Spotlights on Leading Exit Planning Advisors"** are donated to the Global Autism Project:

The Global Autism Project 501(C)3 is a nonprofit organization that provides training to local individuals in evidence-based practice for individuals with autism.

The Global Autism Project believes that every child has the ability to learn, and their potential should not be limited by geographical bounds.

The Global Autism Project seeks to eliminate the disparity in service provision seen around the world by providing high-quality training to individuals providing services in their local community. This training is made sustainable through regular training trips and contiguous remote training.

You can learn more about the Global Autism Project and make direct donations by visiting **GlobalAutismProject.org.**

Contents

A Note to the Reader

Thank you for obtaining your copy of "EXIT SMART Vol. 6: Spotlights on Leading Exit Planning Advisors." This book was originally created as a series of live interviews on my business podcast; that's why it reads like a series of conversations, rather than a traditional book that talks at you.

My team and I have personally invited these professionals to share their knowledge because they have demonstrated that they are true advocates for the success of their clients and have shown their great ability to educate the public on the topic of exiting businesses.

I wanted you to feel as though the participants and I are talking with you, much like a close friend or relative, and felt that creating the material this way would make it easier for you to grasp the topics and put them to use quickly, rather than wading through hundreds of pages.

So relax, grab a pen and paper, take notes, and get ready to learn some fascinating insights from our Leading Exit Planning Advisors.

Warmest regards,

Mark Imperial

Publisher, Author, and Radio Personality

INTRODUCTION

"EXIT SMART Vol. 6: Spotlights on Leading Exit Planning Advisors" is a collaborative book series featuring leading professionals from across the country.

Remarkable Press™ would like to extend a heartfelt thank you to all participants who took the time to submit their chapter and offer their support in becoming ambassadors for this project.

100% of the royalties from this book's retail sales will be donated to the Global Autism Project. Should you want to make a direct donation, visit their website at **GlobalAutismProject.org**

AKILI M. JOHNSON

AKILI M. JOHNSON

Conversation With Akili M. Johnson

Akili, you are a financial advisor with Wells Fargo Advisors. Tell us about your work and the people you help.

Akili M. Johnson: Thank you, Mark, for having me on this morning and for your question about what we do to help people. Over the last few decades of working with families, we have found that trust and performance are essential. This means that our conversations are always 100% confidential, and the focus is on creating value with the services we provide. Our vision is to add the most upside to individuals, families, and business owners we partner with by getting to know them first. We inquire and stay curious about developing the needs of each family we engage by taking a formulaic approach to assist them down the financial highway of life.

Because we look to help our clients who typically own a business that generates revenue from five million and up, what we have found to help these families the most is a team who can help uncover the right information and drive their desired outcome. This is why gathering information is non-negotiable. Our process is simple: get to know the client and produce four to five fundamental reports that increase their business's value, attractiveness, and readiness. We call it our Personal Researched Based Wealth Building Plan, or Personal Wealth Plan for short. Here is what is included:

Personal Wealth Plan - PWP (What Is This?)

- Business Financial Plan including (1) a business valuation, (2) readiness, and (3) attractiveness assessments
- (4) Personal Financial Plan including an estate, investment, and (5) retirement plan

After gathering enough information and creating a PWP, we endure its alignment with their vision, values and goals, and any other unique needs. This information is consistently validated with statements and source documents.

Next is a Strategic Review; we bring in a team of collaborating leaders, for example, Estate and Tax Attorneys; CPAs; and others, to use all the information we have attained to pair with the best strategy. My team handles the implementation and execution of this strategy that the client approves. This is how we help individuals and family business owners by increasing their revenue, maximizing their value, reducing their taxes, and increasing their flexibility of options in the market.

How much thought do business owners put into exit planning?

Akili M. Johnson: Business owners are unique; they have an entrepreneurial focus on an idea and often a lot of passion for their chosen work. The flip side is that the business metrics and numbers are usually less of a focus. The numbers are essential, and all businesses will ultimately transfer. Keeping this in mind, many clients fall short when understanding their true problems. This also extends to other areas that lack the accuracy to determine what their exit will look like. Whatever the case, the business is there to solve many issues and should be integrated into the wealth plan, not separate, as is the case with most business owners. They should know their wealth gap. If you ask what their wealth gap is, many do not know, let alone how their business fits with their wealth goals. Will it fund their wealth plan and their profit and value gaps?

Another area regarding the amount of thought business owners put into exit planning is the non-financial risks. We often see conflict ensue because there's a lot of money changing hands, and someone feels left out. Had that been part of the planning initially, this could have reduced the risk because there are so many variables to address. This is why a team is needed; often, this element is just flat-out missing. Because 70% of business owners are not getting this correct, there's an inflection point in this market right now that allows independent collaboratory advisors to come in and share solutions that can help with funding, private equity, and strategic buyers. It really takes an expert to assess and understand how attractive the business is, what the business owner's wealth is, and what those gaps are so that we can fill them with the proper planning, implementation, and execution.

Where do business owners begin regarding exit planning?

Akili M. Johnson: Business owners should consider their business, personal, and financial goals as a whole. Then see who is most qualified, not just who they like but who has a process and a plan for success, and often this is not the case. Business owners need someone to listen and operate collaboratively. In most cases, it's a team with one person who is the quarterback and is there every step of the way, making them the center of all the strategies to address their vision, values, and goals. They should focus primarily on how the business will fund these other aspects of their life instead of considering the business an extension of their family. They should view it more as a tool to execute their life's work and do what they're passionate about, otherwise known as the next stage of their life, the golden years.

Are there common myths and misconceptions that may hinder owners from selling their businesses?

Akili M. Johnson: We believe business owners are hindered by many misconceptions when selling a business. It ranges from thinking there is only one way to prepare for this process to not knowing what team could be the best fit. Remember, 70% of business owners are unsuccessful in executing this process based on the State of Owner Readiness reports that have been completed. This gives an exit planner the insight to drive the proper solution for a business owner. It ultimately comes down to each business's process and understanding the risk involved. One thing a business owner can do to increase the likelihood they are successful is to ensure there's a lot of cross-pollination between their advisors. And when I say that, what I mean is communication. A lot of times, business owners approach their planning or strategic reviews with just one person. But to do a deep dive and understand the key performance indicators of their business, independent collaboratory advisors are trained to work together as necessary. They should put the client first, keeping the client's needs always top of mind in the solution business.

Our process is holistic, we have consultations, and we're not pushing products because, in most cases, we don't know enough until the intake process is complete. That takes a long time, and many clients are not patient enough because they're so used to someone trying to give them a solution off the top. Business owners need experienced advisors who ask questions and create a unique experience for the families they work with.

However, business owners are typically type A personalities; they want a solution now, but the type of solution they need will take a little more time to uncover what's under the hood of their business. We need to find the right individuals and solutions to implement. And once again, it's the adage of "beginning with the end in mind," taking a look at all of these variables, and not trying to push a product, but trying to understand the business owner's deep concerns by putting them at the center using the expertise of an experienced team to solve for that after we've uncovered all the correct information.

It sounds like an exit planning advisor acts as a ringmaster. Is that correct?

Akili M. Johnson: Mark, you are on it, and typically, yes. We refer to it as a quarterback who works in concert with the other advisors and or teammates uniquely to implement their perspective as a team. As a wealth advisor/planner, I operate as a connecting point to the insurance advisor, estate planner, CPA, business advisor, business coach, and psychology coach. We implement our clients' plans to ensure that when the funds come in, they get diverted to the proper areas that we have already planned for. These plans are customized specifically for each business owner's needs based on their vision, values, and critical goals. We represent those individuals, families, and businesses to provide the best-in-class solution from the beginning to the rest of their journey.

Akili, what inspired you to get started in this field?

Akili M. Johnson: I was a portfolio manager and advisor at a competing firm for many years. It was a top firm in the industry, and most would recognize the name. While there, I primarily worked with retirement clients and offered planning as well. I saw the business changing internally because many banks have their own plans on how they will deliver wealth management. I saw salaries curtailed, and many advisors left for more traditional wealth management platforms.

I've always had an interest in M&A (Mergers & Acquisitions). Upon a lot more research, I realized that there are a lot of dollars changing hands (over about 10 trillion). Chris Snider, president of the Exit Planning Institute, and his son Scott wrote a book called "Walking to Destiny." They talked about the baby boomer generation sunsetting and their inheritors coming in and not having the same passion as their fathers. So I thought it would be a really good way to engage the community. I've always been very interested in helping people within the community. It was a natural space, and this particular approach to business filled a need that may have yet to be understood in the advisor community and markets. I want to be known as a catalyst for that type of change. It involves all my passions: spirit, family, community, health, and education. Those are not just words on a page to me; they encompass my life philosophy. As I add value to business owners, I, too, remain relevant and benefit. That is a win-win scenario.

Is there anything else you would like to share with business owners?

Akili M. Johnson: Find the right advisor who cares about the nuances of your business, personal and financial objectives and uncovers the nuances to ensure the right solution is identified and the business owner gets the most desired outcome. Also, spend more time understanding how to find the correct advisor/ planner. There are a lot of advisors right now who are poaching clients, meaning that they are an expense on the balance sheet, and they're not actually adding value to the business owner. They will happily manage their assets, but they're not helping them generate more revenue.

That's how we differentiate ourselves. We not only have an investment management component, an estate planning component, a business planning component, and a retirement plan component, we focus on the business owner from that vantage point and ensure that we're helping them generate more revenue, decrease their taxes, and increase their options in terms of what they can do in the market. Those are the new-age types of value-centered advisors people should seek. If you have a personal 401k or brokerage account, there will always be advisors or even robo algorithms who will manage those assets because the asset management process is commoditized. But if you're a business owner and you want to take your business to the next level, I would definitely look into collaborating with a value advisor, an exit planning advisor who is on the same side of the balance sheet as the business owner to help them increase revenue, reduce taxes, increase flexibility and let us not forget the financial plan so that they can impact the wealth, profit, and value gaps that are inherent in business.

How can people find you, connect with you, and learn more?

Akili M. Johnson: You can reach me at 214-991-2428. That's my office line, and feel free to email me at a.johnson@wellsfargoadvisors.com. Or visit my website https://home.wellsfargoadvisors.com/a.johnson.

AKILI M. JOHNSON, SE-AWMA®, CEPA®, CPFA®, CFGA®

FINANCIAL ADVISOR
WELLS FARGO ADVISORS | PRIVATE CLIENT GROUP

Akili was born in Rock Island, Illinois. When he was two years old, his family relocated to Houston, Texas, and eventually settled in Richardson, Texas, a few years later. While in school, Akili was an accomplished athlete. During his senior year of high school, Akili was offered a full scholarship to Texas Christian University to play football for Heisman trophy winner Pat Sullivan in 1995. After two years at TCU, Akili transferred to Abilene Christian University to pursue a Financial Management and Accounting degree from the Maybee School of Business.

After graduating from college, Akili embarked upon his successful journey in the financial industry by gaining initial experience as a mortgage broker and retail banking branch manager before moving into wealth management with Merrill Lynch in 2013. His time spent with Citigroup, JPMorgan Chase, Bank of America, and now Wells Fargo Advisors honed the requisite leadership skills that allowed him to lead internal networking groups and expand his own knowledge, experience, and stellar reputation. While taking on these opportunities, Akili continued seeking mentors to assist him with his personal development to be even more effective in helping others realize the power of their own intentional development.

Akili is very dedicated to his community. He routinely donates his time and resources to local boards like Creative Visions Social Services, a non-profit community youth development organization. Akili would describe himself as intellectually curious, energetic, and ultra-positive. He has used his personal philosophy of Spirit, Family, Community, Health, and

Education as a guide to growing and being deliberate in his actions while taking ownership of his life and choices. Akili currently resides in Dallas, Texas, with his wife, Melanie, where they enjoy spending time with family, reading, learning, going to the movies, and working out together.

EMAIL:

akili.johnson@gmail.com

PHONE:

214.991.2428

WEBSITE:

Home.wellsfargoadvisors.com/a.johnson

LINKEDIN:

https://www.linkedin.com/in/akili-m-johnson-cepa®-se-awma®-01157bb

RICK J. KREBS

RICK J. KREBS

Conversation With Rick J. Krebs

Rick, you are an exit planning advisor with Business Sales Group. Tell us about your work and the people you help.

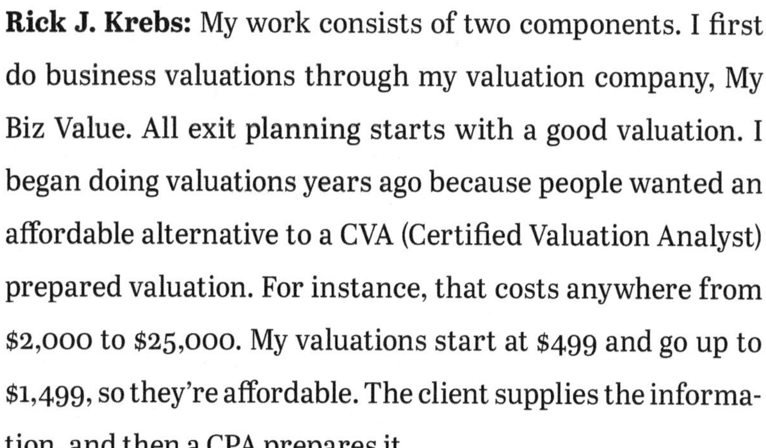

Rick J. Krebs: My work consists of two components. I first do business valuations through my valuation company, My Biz Value. All exit planning starts with a good valuation. I began doing valuations years ago because people wanted an affordable alternative to a CVA (Certified Valuation Analyst) prepared valuation. For instance, that costs anywhere from $2,000 to $25,000. My valuations start at $499 and go up to $1,499, so they're affordable. The client supplies the information, and then a CPA prepares it.

The main thing I do is sell businesses. I also take businesses to market in the M&A space, particularly businesses between $2 million and $30 million enterprise value. That's our sweet spot. We specialize in helping business owners sell their companies for top dollar using innovative, hybrid processes, utilizing the best practices of the business broker and investment banking worlds.

Can you shed some light on the importance of exit planning?

Rick J. Krebs: I am so sold on exit planning that I started the Utah chapter of exit planners. I wrote a book on the subject and have sold businesses for 13 years. In the past, when people wanted to sell, we would run a valuation, and I'd say, "Okay, here's your number." If it wasn't high enough, I would say, "Come back to me in two or three years; let's stay in touch. We'll take you to market when that number hits where you want to be." And honestly, that was not a suitable method of exit planning. It worked. But it was clumsy, so we stumbled through the exit planning process. But now, there are many more tools. Many more people are involved, and it's a revolution sweeping the country consisting of financial planners, wealth managers, CPAs, and M&A advisors, all helping business owners early on to prepare for the exit.

Preparing for a proper exit typically takes two to seven years. I call it "Minding your exit, not blinding your exit." Let's take the time. Let's get it right. Let's create an advisory team to give you the best shot at getting it right because you only have one chance. This is usually the single largest financial transaction of your life.

Can you define "M&A?"

Rick J. Krebs: M&A stands for "Mergers and Acquisitions." Funny enough, my podcast is called "Murders and Accusations" because often we kill it, and other times deals are killed. Typically, business brokers handle transactions of $2 million and under and do a great job. They blast out the listing to multiple sources. Investment bankers usually tackle transactions of $30 million and above. They run a bid process and do competitive bidding to create competition and increase prices. Then there's that space in between, which is the mergers and acquisitions space, consisting of businesses that are $2 million to $30 million in value, which are small potatoes to the bankers, larger than what most brokers do, and entail a more sophisticated process.

What do business owners need to know when considering selling?

Rick J. Krebs: When you start your business, consider an exit. It's never too early to plan. I talked to a business owner the other day, and we just completed his valuation. He said, "Well, do I really want to go through what I need to do to prepare for an exit?" I said, "Absolutely." And here's why. Exit planning helps you build your business. The business principles used to plan for an exit are solid business principles, period. So you can plan for that exit and build your business to the point where you won't exit. Either way, it's a win-win. You're going to build such a great business that you want to keep it, or you're going to build such a great business that it will be more attractive and valuable when you sell.

What are some common pitfalls that sabotage a successful exit?

Rick J. Krebs: The first one is you must plan for your exit. We can sell your company, but you must monitor how much gas is in your tank. Are you blinking on empty? Where are your energy levels for the business? You don't want to wait until you're out of energy to run the business because then the business goes downhill, becoming a very different sale at a significantly lower price. So guard your energy levels. If you are losing energy now, it's best to start thinking about an exit before you run out of gas and give it away.

Secondly, you must have a team of people, including an exit planner and an M&A advisor, who can help you prepare months in advance. The earlier you start, the better. We had a company the other day on a cash basis. Typically these companies consist of a spouse doing the books at the kitchen table at night. Soon, they go from $100,000 to $1 million in revenue and then become a $10 million business, but the financial records have not become sophisticated along with the business. So they end up with some work to do. It's hard to go back and do that work; it's much easier moving forward.

Lastly, look at your business operationally. Get a formal valuation done to look at your business through a buyer's eye. They look at it entirely differently than you do as a business owner. All you're doing is paying the bills, keeping customers happy, and making payroll. You're working *in* the business rather than *on* the business. A formal valuation will help you understand the metrics that will increase your value. We typically experience "aha" moments with owners during valuation engagements. "Wow, so you mean for every additional dollar I put towards my EBITDA, I get four times the amount on my value?!" Or they are a C Corp, and because of double taxation, we talk to them about making an S selection. These issues come up at formal valuations so that we can get ahead of them.

Rick, what inspired you to get started in this field?

Rick J. Krebs: Let's start with how I began selling businesses. I sold a business, didn't have any help, got clobbered, and we had to get attorneys to get paid. I sold the business the wrong way. That's how I learned. You learn more from your mistakes than you do from your successes. I said, "I won't allow people to make that mistake. My clients are going to learn how to do it right. We're going to help them do it the right way." That's how I got into the business of selling businesses.

My exit planning journey was different. I realized a few years ago that clients needed to start earlier to prepare for selling their businesses. I'd been selling businesses for eight years and thought, "This is working, but it's clunky. It needs to be better. We're leaving money on the table for buyers and sellers." What could we do for your retirement if you make a $15 million exit compared to a $5 million exit? It's an entirely different lifestyle. I realized that we could move the needle exponentially, not just incrementally, with the sale, and exit planning was the key.

I wrote a book and decided I wanted to be an influencer. I want to help people sell their businesses by design, not by default, by educating them about the process, pitfalls, and who they need on their team. I also started the Utah chapter of exit planners and became a Certified Exit Planning Advisor. Our group is not competitive; it's collaborative. I'm proud to be a CEPA in this group, educating ourselves to educate our clients better and prepare them for a better exit.

Is there anything else you would like to share with business owners?

Rick J. Krebs: I will share a little story about something I recently learned. This is a story about a baby rattlesnake. There was a hiker, and he was going up a hill. At the bottom of the hill, there was this baby rattlesnake on the side of the road, and it was all stretched out and limp because it was cold. The hiker said, "Oh, you're so cute. You're a baby." The rattlesnake said, "You know what I am? I'm cold and need to be taken to the top of the mountain to sit on a warm rock in the sun. Will you take me to the top of the mountain?" The hiker said, "But you're a rattlesnake. I don't want to risk it." The rattlesnake said, "I promise I won't bite you." So the hiker carefully picked up the baby rattlesnake, carried it to the top of the mountain, and set it on a rock. As he set it down, the rattlesnake bit him on the hand. The hiker exclaimed, "Ouch! You said you wouldn't bite me!" And the rattlesnake said, "Yes, but you knew what I was when you picked me up."

So if I could say one thing to business owners, it's don't pick up baby rattlesnakes. If you have an advisor or advisors who have been with you for years but aren't getting you what you need, it's time to let them go and find the right team. I tell you that story because you need advisors such as a mergers & acquisitions advisor (not murders & accusations), CPA, attorneys, wealth manager, and financial planner who align with your values. Are rattlesnakes important? Yes, they kill mice; however, you want to avoid having rattlesnakes on your team. You want people who you will mesh with. You're going to have to make some tough decisions. It might mean you have to fire a CPA or an advisor, but creating a team you can work well with is imperative..

How can people find you, connect with you, and learn more?

Rick J. Krebs: You can find us at www.Bsalesgroup.com. Find my book at www.designmysale.com or on Amazon titled "Sell Your Business By Design, Not By Default." For valuations, visit www.mybizvalue.com. You can reach me by phone at 801-688-2554, or you can email me at rick@bsalesgroup.com.

RICK J. KREBS, CPA, CEPA, M&A ADVISOR

Business Sales Group and My Biz Value

After getting a BS and MAcc in accounting from Utah State University, Rick started his career in public accounting as a CPA. As an entrepreneur at heart, he tired of "counting other people's money" after three years and endeavored to start making money on his own. He founded and successfully ran a mortgage company and sold it without any help. This was a disaster, and he learned how *not* to sell a business. Vowing not to let that bad experience happen to other business owners, he started Business Sales Group, a Mergers & Acquisitions advisory firm.

BSG specializes in helping business owners sell their companies for top dollar using innovative, hybrid processes, utilizing the best practices of the business broker and investment banking worlds. Rick has been featured in FORBES and is the bestselling author of “Sell Your Business By Design Not By Default.” Rick is the President and Co-founder of the EPI Utah Chapter of Exit Planners, a group of professionals who advise business owner clients on the sale of their business and exit planning in preparation for an exit. You can listen to Rick on his podcast: “M&A Murders & Accusations - How to Not Kill the Sale of Your Business,” on Spotify and iTunes and visit his YouTube channel.

Due to repeated requests from clients looking for an affordable business valuation, Rick founded My Biz Value, a business valuation company. These valuations are used for exit planning, selling a business, taxes, partner buy-outs, divorces, etc., and start at only $499.

When not selling businesses, Rick is a cowboy and can be found with his family working on his ranch or with his horses riding the trails of the western U.S.

EMAIL:

Rick@bsalesgroup.com

PHONE:

801-688-2554

WEBSITE:

www.Bsalesgroup.com

OTHER:

www.MyBizValue.com for valuations

PAUL MORETTI

PAUL MORETTI

Conversation With Paul Moretti

Paul, you are an exit planning advisor with Cerity Partners. Tell us about your work and the people you help.

Paul Moretti: We specialize in assisting privately held companies. While exiting a business may be the end goal, our focus is building value in the business, which centers around many components. The goal is to build and maximize the value of the business at all times. That way, if the owner is required to sell or should want to sell, they will be in a position to obtain the highest possible selling price.

There are several factors for the owner to consider. What is the value of your business today? What do you want to do in your personal life? What are the financial resources required to accomplish your personal goals? What is the value of the business necessary to meet the financial resources requirement?

One of the most often overlooked aspects by the owner is not considering and planning for what they want to do outside the business and in the next chapter of their life upon exiting the business. Exit planning is a process that should begin the moment you start a business. It's all about ensuring you accomplish your personal, financial, and business goals, maximizing the business's value, and controlling the outcome so you can exit on your terms.

How much thought do business owners put into exit planning?

Paul Moretti: In my experience, they don't think much about it or plan at all. We are generally contacted when an owner receives an unsolicited offer for their business. At this point, the owner has yet to devote time or effort to the planning process. In fact, statistics show that between 70% and 80% of business owners regret their decision to sell a year later because they didn't plan for what was next. It wasn't that they didn't like the price that they received. It's more about not planning for their life after owning the business and developing financial plans to ensure they have enough money to accomplish their personal goals.

Exit planning is a continuous assessment and evaluation of the owner's personal, financial, and business goals. The owner should ask themselves daily, "What's the value of my business? Have I maximized that value? Do I want to continue to grow the business? Do I want to exit the business?" Exiting a business takes some time as well, much longer than most people anticipate.

Are there common pitfalls that can sabotage a successful exit?

Paul Moretti: The value of the business is based on what someone is willing to pay for the company rather than what the owner believes it is worth. The buyer will examine the financials and evaluate intangible assets, such as employees, customers, infrastructure, and social aspects. Does the company have qualified people? Are the right people in the right seats? Are the staff educated on the customers and the market? Are employees well trained? Can employees make decisions, or does the business owner make all decisions? What is the extent of customer relationships? Are they long-term?

Are they contractual? Are those customers transferable or solely reliant on the business owner?

A buyer will also look at your intellectual property, technology, processes, and systems. Are those documented? Are they in a manner such that somebody can acquire and repurpose them? What is the company's brand? Is the business only identified with the owner? What is the culture of the organization?

All of these considerations reflect the business risk for the acquirer. A higher risk assessment can translate into a lower offer price and a more extended earn-out period.

Paul, what inspired you to get started in this field?

Paul Moretti: I was the CFO of a few different organizations. I found this opportunity to use my CFO experience to help business owners. I obtained my certification as an exit planner to better assist my clients. What I've learned and what excites me is helping business owners understand it's not just about the exit itself. It's about maximizing and building value in your business every single day. It's about risk protection, protecting what you've built, and protecting yourself from a divorce, a disagreement with a partner, death, disability, or distress.

It's fun for me to offer a comprehensive planning approach. It requires a team of professionals, such as a value advisor like myself, a CPA, a tax accountant, a financial advisor, a financial planner, an estate planner, a banker, and an M&A advisor. An entire team of professionals needs to be involved in the process for a successful exit, and I enjoy working with and learning from the other experts.

Is there anything else you would like to share with business owners?

Paul Moretti: Business owners rarely know the value of their business. They may think they know because they heard a number from a friend who recently sold, but they need to approach value from the lens of the buyer and look at all of the intangible assets I mentioned.

The other issue is starting too late with a plan. Business owners often receive an offer and want to move forward with the sale. However, they need to take a step back and consider if they want to strike a deal with the first person who offers or thoroughly evaluate the business to determine the best course of action.

Non-financial aspects of selling the company should also be considered. The owner may be a pillar in the community and view their employees as a family. Understanding the different types of buyers and what each means for your business, employees, and community is critical. The highest bidder may eliminate employees and move some or all operations to another community. Obtaining the highest possible purchase price may not align with the owner's values.

How can people find you, connect with you, and learn more?

Paul Moretti: I can be reached by email at pmoretti@ceritypartners.com or by phone at 502-882-4150. My LinkedIn profile is www.linkedin.com/in/pauljmoretti/.

PAUL MORETTI, CEPA

PRINCIPAL
CERITY PARTNERS

Paul is a Principal in the Louisville office of Cerity Partners. He provides CFO, advisory, valuation, and exit planning services to privately-held businesses and non-profit organizations.

Before joining Cerity Partners, Paul served as CFO for companies in the financial services and manufacturing industries.

Paul is a Certified Exit Planning and CPA (inactive).

EMAIL:
pmoretti@ceritypartners.com

PHONE:
502-882-4150

WEBSITE:
ceritypartners.com

LINKEDIN:
www.linkedin.com/in/pauljmoretti/

ERIC COOPER

ERIC COOPER

Conversation With Eric Cooper

Eric, you are the founder of Sooner Business Advisors. Tell us about your work and the people you help.

Eric Cooper: We demystify exit planning for business owners. How you run your business is inextricably linked to how you exit your business. And one thing is true for everybody: at some point, whether by will or by force, you will no longer be able to run your business. But many of us want our businesses to outlast us. So how do we solve that problem? How do we solve the retirement problem? How do we solve the transition problem?

I help business owners manage all those interrelated decisions between three main areas, the personal, the business, and the financial, to create their desired outcomes ultimately. They may exit internally or externally or graduate from being an owner-operator to an executive investor. There are many ways to do it.

I'm an entrepreneur, and I started my first business at 15, a mobile auto detailing business. I learned more about business during that experience than anything I've done after. I've owned a couple of businesses between now and then. I think like an entrepreneur; I genuinely relate to entrepreneurs and like solving their problems.

How much thought do business owners put into exit planning?

Eric Cooper: The exit planning industry is only 10 to 15 years old. Some lone wolves did it before then, but having a codified industry and certifications to show competency is relatively new. So nine out of ten owners I talk to have never even thought about this and have never spoken to anybody claiming to do exit planning.

Business owners prefer to avoid talking about it. Exiting a business equals the death of their identity. Lower middle market business owners drive our economy, work hard to make their dreams come alive, and derive extreme pride from providing for their employees and families. The skill sets they have developed are a core part of who they are. Naturally, any thought of divorcing the business is repulsive to them. It's much easier to do what they know how to do, which is run the business day to day, be profitable, take care of people, have an excellent reputation in the community, and not deal with the inevitable problem that eventually they're going to have some transition in their lives. We provide the clarity to bring that transition on their own timeline and terms.

A common misconception is that exit planning means planning to sell your business. That is one exit option. There are two different exit pathways, internal and external. And even further, there are multiple pathways within those two categories you can choose, including blended options. Sometimes it's a full transition. Sometimes it's a partial or gradual transition. We are exit option agnostic at Sooner Business Advisors. All we're doing is bringing the future into the present so that owners can do something about it now, bringing that transition into their own timeline and terms.

I'll give you one poignant statistic from the National Exit Planning Institute. 72% of business owners who transition from a CEO or majority stakeholder share regret it within 12 months. And in the survey, almost none of the regret had to do with the money they received for the business. It all had to do with personal identity being divorced. That's why we focus on the personal, the business, and the financial, and the series of sequential and interrelated decisions that allow an owner to use the right professionals, have someone who knows how to manage a professional team and create the most meaningful outcomes that they want to see in their lives. The owner is the client; the business is not the client.

Why was exit planning created?

Eric Cooper: We are in the midst of the most significant transfer of wealth in American history because of the boomer generation. There were so many of them and so much competition. They owned businesses as a percentage more than any other generation in American history. Boomers "are their work" and identify very closely with it, unlike Gen Z, Gen X, and millennials, who don't find as much personal identity in their work.

Post-boomers, things like the luxury economy and the cost of a bachelor's degree exploded. So people carry a lot more debt. Nowadays, people don't necessarily find their identity in work and don't work as long as the boomers did. People are less entrepreneurially inclined because of the rising cost of living and dual-income families and the explosion of the luxury economy. It's mainly been about climbing the corporate ranks, paying off your school debt, and getting a good job. So there are many profitable businesses that, quite frankly, folks like me, and you aren't in the position to buy. That's why you see all the consolidation in private equity firms. That's why these industries have so many strategic buyouts and consolidations. There aren't folks capable of running businesses or interested in running businesses with the capital means to buy.

So how do we solve that problem? That was the impetus in the late 90s when this seed started growing. Some fathers of the exit planning industry, like John Leonetti, John Dini, Peter Christman, and Chris Snider, helped codify this industry and the professional certifications around it so that a guy like myself, who's been interested in this since I was 15, can start bringing value to business owners. To do exit planning and transition planning correctly, the number one thing you need is to have somebody who understands the framework and how all the pieces interact, not necessarily a micro advisor.

You can have your investment managers, business brokers, tax people, legal people, and insurance people, but when was the last time you had all of these advisors sitting in the same room talking about your aspirations and meaningful outcomes? It's my job to coordinate all that expertise and advice in a hierarchy and sequence in a project management style to ensure we can actualize those meaningful outcomes. Generally speaking, business owners say that's never happened within their team of advisors, and they certainly don't often feel equipped to be an effective general of that brigade. We create the "board of directors" experience to match the life goals of the business owner, whether they're looking to retire or exit two or 15 years from now or it's just an idea. Exit planning is just good business strategy.

Eric, what inspired you to get started in this field?

Eric Cooper: The first thing I mentioned was the business I started when I was 15. When I was researching what business I wanted to start, I was considering my skill set and what would need the least amount of capital because I was working at an amusement park making $7.25 an hour. I wasn't rolling in the dough, and I needed some money. So I went to a couple of friends and pitched the idea to them. They gave me a few bucks, and I brought my brother in as a silent partner. Even as I was making those decisions on what business I wanted to start, if I wanted partners or not, and how much ownership would work over the thing we were building that wasn't even worth anything yet, I had the mindset of wanting it to have value so I could eventually sell it.

We all know those business owners who work 70 hours a week and are miserable inside a cage that they built around themselves. They're not independent of the business. I observed that growing up and didn't want that to be the case for me. So when I was looking to build my first business, I was already considering the exit plan before registering the DBA. That's just always been the way that I've worked and operated.

When I was made aware of this as an industry and some of the certifications that exist in it, it just immediately spoke to me because these are the conversations I have anyway. I thought, "Wait, I can make a career out of this?!" And so from there, I received the certifications, built a business model around it, and paired it with my financial planning practice, which I still do for business owners and clients. It just made too much sense, and I'm too passionate about the work not to do it.

Is there anything else you would like to share with business owners?

Eric Cooper: Many business owners think, "I can see how exit planning will apply to my business *at some point*. But right now, I'm 36 years old, I have a profitable business, and it's not a conversation for me to have. Maybe 20 years from now."

If there's one thing you take away from this conversation, understand that exit planning is simply good business strategy. For example, my retirement planning clients are talking about retirement, even when they're 30 or 40 years old. Even if we're looking at something 20 to 30 years down the line, all we're doing is planning with the end in mind. We're taking the future and bringing it into the present so that we can do something about it now. So if you want to graduate your level of business ownership, or you just want to run a business that has maximum harvestable value, and you have no idea when you're going to exit, but you want to make sure that your eventual exit is on your timeline and terms, and you've got a profitable, growing business, this conversation is for you. It sounds different than somebody looking to sell their business in two years or transfer it to employees or children. I work incredibly well with those owners too, and much of the firepower in my company and our industry is designed to help those owners design, execute, and thrive through a high value transition. But at the end of the day, the same concepts that drive that person's ability to have a successful exit are the same concepts that allow you to maximize profitability, maximize your quality of life, and bring your future exit on your own timeline and terms now, even if it's not something that's in the imminent future. The exit planning conversation is for you if you run a successful growing business and want to graduate to the next level.

How can people find you, connect with you, and learn more?

Eric Cooper: My website is www.soonerbusinessadvisors.com. You can find information about my partners there and me. My email is eric.cooper@soonerbusinessadvisors.com. I love having conversations. I'm a people person. I try my best to get personally back to everyone who sends me a message.

ERIC COOPER,
CERTIFIED EXIT PLANNING ADVISOR, FINANCIAL PLANNER

FOUNDER
SOONER BUSINESS ADVISORS

Eric serves entrepreneurs because he is one. Since starting his first business as a mobile auto detailing service at 15 years old, Eric has held roles in banking, insurance, wealth management, business planning and consulting, enterprise value creation, and integrated financial planning. Eric has been privileged to work with a diverse landscape of clients, including professional athletes, successful entrepreneurs and their families, and more.

True planning is two modes simultaneously: First, a skilled orchestration of the big picture framework, with total clarity of values and meaningful outcomes. Second, the ongoing management of sequence, priority, and execution of the interrelated decisions and projects along the way to actualize those meaningful future outcomes. As a distinguished Certified Exit Planning Advisor, Eric simplifies the complex so owners can write their own stories with intention. He works with owners across the country to 1) Align their personal, business, and financial values, 2) Build and quarterback the right multidisciplinary professional board to best serve them, 3) Implement the Value Acceleration Methodology to unlock the most transferable value, income, and impact from their business, 4) Execute high value, successful transitions from their businesses, and 5) Work with them for the long term after the successful exit to achieve their most meaningful potential.

Owners deserve advisors who view them as the client, making their fulfilled vision the true measure of success, not business-centric advisors who view the business as their client and keep score only on the spreadsheets. Owner-centricity is a core Sooner Business Advisors pledge because there's no such thing as a "standard case" when it comes to people.

Eric is a passionate hunter and angler, always traveling in pursuit of wild places. He is also an avid sports fan, podcaster, and culinarian. He lives with his wife and four children in Londonderry, New Hampshire.

EMAIL:

eric.cooper@soonerbusinessadvisors.com

PHONE:

603-321-6531

WEBSITE:

www.soonerbusinessadvisors.com

KELLY BERENBAUM

KELLY BERENBAUM

Conversation With Kelly Berenbaum

Kelly, you are the founder of Blue Tree Financial. Tell us about your work and the people you help.

Kelly Berenbaum: Blue Tree Financial is a flat-fee financial planning and investment management firm, meaning we get paid for the services we deliver and not a percentage of the assets we manage. We offer comprehensive financial planning, investment management, and business succession planning to business owners and their families. What makes us slightly different is that we focus on the owner's personal objectives and look for creative solutions. We do not come in with a preconceived notion about whether to sell the business or transition it to family or employees. We have found this approach comforting to owners who have felt pressure to create a "liquidity event" when they first want to understand all the options and get comfortable with tradeoffs. From the business perspective, offering a flat fee arrangement removes conflicts and helps build trust that the advice is related to the business, not the succession path they choose.

We also serve corporate employees who may need comprehensive financial planning and may not have access to traditional advisors because a large concentration of their wealth is invested in their company retirement plans.

How much thought do business owners put into exit planning?

Kelly Berenbaum: Many business owners are so busy in their business's day-to-day management and growth that they're not really thinking about what exiting means, either personally or professionally. If they exit the business, what will they do with their time? What are they going to do on a day-to-day basis? What do they need to get from the business financially, whether transitioning to the next generation or selling externally, to support themselves and their families into retirement and beyond?

Looking internally at the business, do they have a management team in place so they can step away and delegate day-to-day operations? Do they have the operational and administrative processes and outside support from partners and vendors to keep things stable from an accounting perspective? Is everything clean, smooth, and easily transitioned to the new owner and/or the next generation?

The key is the mindset. What do they need to do personally to envision the next chapter of their lives? All other aspects follow in terms of planning, but the personal piece is the most challenging, particularly in environments like we're facing now. Everyone is nervous about the economy and what will happen. So I find business owners retrenching and concentrating on running the business, which can cause them to lose sight of their succession goals. And that is important, but maintaining that big picture on the architecture of your personal and business life and carefully making strategic choices is also essential.

Are there common mistakes business owners make regarding exiting?

Kelly Berenbaum: Business owners must realize that they will have to exit at some point, which might not always be in their control. So the more action they take now, the more plans they put in place, and the more they have solidified their business, the better chance they will be making the decision when it's time to exit - as opposed to some external force. That's the biggest challenge.

The next challenge is staying the course. Once we've outlined a plan and started moving in that direction, let's keep going! Of course, adjustments will need to be made along the way, but let's continue to keep sight of the goal.

When is the best time to start exit planning?

Kelly Berenbaum: In a perfect world, begin planning the moment you start your business. What is this business going to do for you and your family? And how are you going to transition? But realistically, around ten years from when you want to exit your business will give you the most control. Five years out is still good, but you have less time to react to external things like market conditions. Five to ten years is a healthy range for you to think through all the implications, put your plan in place, and begin executing.

Kelly, what inspired you to get started in this field?

Kelly Berenbaum: I love financial planning. I love the architecture of financial solutions. I spent most of my career behind a computer. And I still do to some extent, so I am fascinated by and get a lot of personal fulfillment in working with small business owners in various industries. For example, some of my clients work in the construction industry, creating beautiful structures that will potentially be enjoyed for generations to come. Regardless of the industry, I enjoy learning about all the creative ways they are building their businesses and using my expertise to help them build upon their success throughout their lifetime.

Is there anything else you would like to share with business owners?

Kelly Berenbaum: There is a lot of common sense that is not common knowledge. Think about what you want your post-business life to be realistically for yourself and your family. Consider where your business is today and where it needs to be to optimize that vision. And then get started. Engage the help of professionals where you need it, but get moving in that direction.

How can people find you, connect with you, and learn more?

Kelly Berenbaum: You can visit my website, www.bluetreefi.com, to schedule a complimentary consultation or call me at 407-434-1616.

Content is for education only and does not constitute financial, legal, or tax advice. Please consult a professional as needed.

Certified Financial Planner Board of Standards, Inc. (CFP Board) owns the CFP® certification mark, the CERTIFIED FINANCIAL PLANNER™ certification mark, and the CFP® certification mark (with plaque design) logo in the United States, which it authorizes use of by individuals who successfully complete CFP Board's initial and ongoing certification requirements.

KELLY BERENBAUM, CFP®, CEPA®

FOUNDER AND LEAD PLANNER
BLUE TREE FINANCIAL LLC

After a successful career on the corporate side of financial services in technology, product leadership, and client strategy roles, Kelly founded Blue Tree Financial LLC, a flat-fee financial planning firm. Kelly provides personal financial planning, investment management, and succession planning for family business owners. She also serves high earners who embrace the importance of a financial plan but may not have assets to invest, either because they are invested in an employer-qualified plan or are still early in building their assets.

Kelly enjoys using her knowledge and skills to collaborate with and co-create financial solutions with her clients. She particularly enjoys complex, multi-faceted plans where there may be more than one path to success.

Kelly is a CFP® professional and holds the Certified Exit Planning Advisor credential or CEPA®. CFP® professionals have met rigorous financial planning qualifications and agreed to abide by the standards set forth in the CFP Board's Code of Ethics and Standards of Conduct. A Certified Exit Planning Advisor or CEPA® is a holistic business advisor who helps a business owner align business, personal, and financial goals while building transferable value into their business so that the owner is always prepared to capitalize on a transition of their company, planned or unplanned.

Kelly holds a Bachelor of Arts degree in International Business from Eckerd College and a Master of Business Administration degree from the University of South Florida.

EMAIL:

info@bluetreefi.com

PHONE:

407-434-1616

WEBSITE:

https://bluetreefi.com/

LINKEDIN COMPANY PAGE:

https://www.linkedin.com/company/blue-tree-financial/

LINKEDIN PERSONAL PAGE:

https://www.linkedin.com/in/kelly-berenbaum/

LINDA A. HAMILTON

LINDA A. HAMILTON

Conversation With Linda A. Hamilton

Linda, you are a CPA and exit planning advisor. Tell us about your work and the people you help.

Linda A. Hamilton: As a CPA and exit planning advisor, I've had the privilege of working with business owners for over 30 years, helping them achieve their financial and business goals. It's been an incredible journey so far, and I'm excited to continue supporting clients with services like one-page business plan workshops. These workshops help clients stay focused and aligned with their vision, which is key to achieving success.

As an exit planning advisor, I collaborate with business owners at all stages of the exit planning process. From those who are just starting to explore their options to those who are actively preparing to sell or transfer ownership, I love being able to provide guidance and support. And I have a special place in my heart for women-owned businesses, as they face unique challenges and opportunities.

Speaking of exit planning, it's something that's incredibly important for all business owners to consider. Even if you're not planning to sell or transfer ownership anytime soon, unexpected events can happen, and it's best to be prepared. In fact, did you know that unforeseen events prompt 55% of all exits? By taking a proactive approach to exit planning, business owners can achieve their personal and financial goals and create a lasting legacy. So, if you haven't started thinking about your exit strategy, now's the time to do it!

How much thought do business owners put into exit planning?

Linda A. Hamilton: You know, it's surprising how many business owners haven't given exit planning much thought. They put it on the back burner and don't realize the consequences until it's too late. Many don't even have a plan in place, which can be a huge problem down the line.

If you wait until you're ready to sell or leave your business, you could be in for a rude awakening. Did you know that only 20%

or less of listed businesses get sold? That's a pretty staggering statistic. Trying to make a quick exit is far from ideal, as there won't be enough time to build up the value of your business.

That's why I always encourage my clients to start thinking about exit planning early on. It's never too soon to start developing a plan and working on ways to increase your income and growth. I call it the "GPS" System - Grow, Profit, and Scale. By focusing on these three things, business owners can proactively prepare for their eventual exit and increase their chances of a successful transition. At the end of the day, it's all about achieving your desired outcomes and leaving a lasting legacy.

Are there common pitfalls that can sabotage a successful exit?

Linda A. Hamilton: Building a business from the ground up is a labor of love. Entrepreneurs pour their hearts, souls, and life savings into creating something they can be proud of. But a lot of them don't realize that they need to think about the next step, too. Unfortunately, many business owners who exit their businesses end up unhappy within two years post-sale. And, often, it's not because they didn't get a good deal.

It's because they didn't have the personal side of their plan mapped out.

Things like retirement lifestyle and how much money they'll need to maintain their desired quality of life are essential to consider. On the business side, if only 20% of listed businesses end up selling, the remaining 80% have some tough questions to answer about what happens next.

There's the fate of the owner's family, customers, vendors, suppliers, and all the relationships they've built over time. Even if a business looks attractive to potential buyers, it can still be devalued during the due diligence process for various reasons, like being too owner-dependent or lacking essential contracts. Sometimes the systems and processes aren't nearly as well documented as the owner thought.

And here's the kicker: Over 50% of exits are unplanned due to unexpected events. Burnout, family responsibilities, illness, legal issues, and unstable market conditions can force a business owner to exit earlier than planned. That's why I prioritize ensuring that my clients, especially the women I work with, don't become part of these statistics.

Unanticipated events can happen at any time, and business owners must be able to control their exit and the outcome as much as possible when the time comes. That's where my expertise comes in. By helping business owners proactively plan their exits and considering all the angles, I can help them achieve their desired outcomes and leave a lasting legacy.

When is the best time to begin exit planning?

Linda A. Hamilton: Many entrepreneurs wait until they're close to selling their business to start thinking about exit planning. But that's not the best approach. At our firm, we focus on three critical areas regarding exit planning. First, is the business attractive to a potential buyer? Second, is the business exit-ready? And third, is the owner personally and financially ready for an exit?

I always recommend that entrepreneurs start planning with the end in mind right from the beginning. They should consider whether they'll sell, transfer the business to a family member or employees, or merge with another company. Exit planning is just good business strategy. It ensures you're profitable, have good cash flow, and can get the most money for your business when ready to exit. And here's an analogy for you: Getting hurricane insurance doesn't increase the likelihood of a hurricane! Similarly, exit planning is all about legacy protection. It ensures that all the hard work and assets you put into your business will result in a soft landing for you and your loved ones later.

During the growth phase, many entrepreneurs often focus on top-line revenues and minimizing taxable profits. And while that might be good tax planning, it can actually make it harder to obtain loans and devalue the business in the long run. After years of building a business, an owner may have anywhere from 50 to 90% of their wealth tied up in it. That's why it's crucial to ensure that all your advisors are on the same page and supporting you in achieving your long-term goals for the future.

Linda, what inspired you to get started in this field?

Linda A. Hamilton: Well, I've always been passionate about entrepreneurship and helping business owners achieve their goals. In fact, I'm a business owner and a member of several organizations that serve business owners. But the one close to my heart is The Women Presidents Organization. It's a peer advisory group that meets once a month, and it's been an incredible experience being a part of it.

As a group of 20 business owners, we brainstorm, problem-solve in roundtables, and discuss challenges. And over the years, the topic of selling a business and transitioning has come up quite frequently. It's not uncommon for business owners to reach a point where they

feel burned out and no longer want to continue, even if their company is successful. And when that happens, many of them don't know where to start when it comes to selling their business. I've seen this recurring issue happen far too often, which inspired me to incorporate exit planning into my services.

As a CPA, it just made sense to me, and I knew it would be a valuable addition to my clients. My approach to exit planning is from a coaching and educational perspective rather than executing the exit itself. That way, business owners can come to me before they're ready to work with a broker or investment banker. I guide them through the process and help them prepare for the next steps in their exit journey. It's been an incredibly fulfilling experience for me, and I'm honored to be able to help many business owners achieve their goals and leave a lasting legacy.

Is there anything else you would like to share with business owners?

Linda A. Hamilton: All business owners should keep a couple of things in mind. First and foremost, make sure that your systems and processes are well-documented. It might not seem like the most exciting thing in the world, but trust me, it's crucial. When it comes time to sell your business, having all the necessary documentation for due diligence can make all the difference. And not having the right documentation? That can seriously devalue your business or cause the deal to fall through entirely. Nobody wants that, right?

Secondly, I recommend that all business owners take some self-scoring assessments to evaluate their business's current state. It's like an annual business health check! Do you know how you routinely get checkups for your body? Well, your business needs the same kind of attention. You've got to remove those rose-colored glasses and be honest with yourself about where your business stands. It's important to give yourself time to identify your business's potential worth and concentrate on increasing its value over time.

If you want to get started, you can actually score your business for free on my website at growprofitscale.com. These small but crucial steps will help you prepare for a successful exit and ensure you make the most of all your hard work and dedication. Trust me; it's worth it in the end!

How can people find you, connect with you, and learn more?

Linda A. Hamilton: People can find me and learn more about our services by visiting our two websites that cater to business owners: https://www.growprofitscale.com and https://www.lahcpas.com. You can also connect with me and see my professional background on my LinkedIn profile. I always joke that if you Google me, you might come across the actress who starred in "The Terminator." My CPA firm is called Linda A. Hamilton, CPA LLC, where we terminate tax and business challenges. Please feel free to reach out, and I am happy to help you with your exit planning needs or answer any questions you might have.

For Educational and Informational Purposes Only
The information contained in this book and any related resources are for educational and informational purposes only.

Not Accounting, Tax, or Other Professional Advice
The information contained in this book and any related resources is not intended as, and shall not be understood or construed as, legal, financial, tax, or other professional advice. While the professional is a licensed CPA and CEPA, the information contained in this book is not a substitute for accounting or tax advice from a licensed accountant or other professional who is aware of the facts and circumstances of your individual situation.

LINDA A. HAMILTON, CPA, CEPA, CGMA, CPBA, SYSTEMologist™

GROW PROFIT SCALE LLC,
A DIVISION OF LINDA A HAMILTON, CPA LLC

Meet Linda A. Hamilton - she's a business guru with over 30 years of experience, and she's passionate about helping female entrepreneurs succeed. Linda's mission is to empower business owners by providing them with the tools and knowledge they need to build profitable and resilient companies.

She does this through a range of services, including workshops, assessments, and her comprehensive Grow, Profit, Scale system.

Linda's services are designed to help businesses align their goals with their personal and business vision. Her business assessments are a popular starting point for business owners who want to explore their options for a future sale. With Linda's help, these assessments provide a score for their current status and an actionable plan for improvement.

Aside from her consulting work, Linda is also a sought-after speaker on topics such as business and tax planning, financial fluency, and budgeting. She's an expert in succession planning and the use of simple business plans as a roadmap for growth.

When she's not busy running her firm, Linda enjoys leisurely activities like walking, reading mysteries, putting together 3,000-piece jigsaw puzzles, and binge-watching TV shows with her husband. She's also a dedicated volunteer preschool teacher with 25 years of experience, which makes her particularly patient when explaining complex tax and accounting concepts to business owners.

Linda is an award-winning Certified Public Accountant, Certified SYSTEMologist™, Certified Exit Planner (CEPA), a

Maus Accredited Partner, and Chapter Co-President of the Institute of Advisors. She's an active member of several professional associations, including AICPA, NYSSCPAs, Women Presidents Organization, Woodard Alliance, Exit-Planning Institute, and Enterprising Women Magazine's Advisory Board. The firm is also a WBENC-certified woman-owned company.

She splits her time between Fort Lauderdale and Manhattan, and she's always ready to help entrepreneurs achieve their dreams.

EMAIL:

lhamilton@growprofitscale.com

PHONE:

212-850-2521

WEBSITE:

https://growprofitscale.com

LINKEDIN:

https://www.linkedin.com/in/lindahamiltoncpa/

KYLE BOCHAT

KYLE BOCHAT

CONVERSATION WITH KYLE BOCHAT

Kyle, you are a Certified Exit Planning Advisor. Tell us about your work and the people you help.

Kyle Bochat: I wear a couple of hats. My primary roles, which I've been doing the longest, are financial planning, wealth management, and portfolio design. Over the years, I have grown my practice to work with many entrepreneurs. Entrepreneurs tend to do very well financially and easily fit my profile as an ideal client. But one of the most significant issues we've encountered in financial planning for entrepreneurs is helping them understand the value of their business, its growth potential, and how that fits with everything else we traditionally look at in financial planning. For many owners I work with, their net worth is made up primarily of equity in their business, not 401ks, stocks, bonds, and funds.

Clearly, guessing at the value of the business or taking an owner's word for it can completely derail good financial planning if incorrect. It became critical to add this line of service to my practice along with the appropriate tools, resources, and professionals needed to help business owners successfully plan their future and exit. Becoming a Certified Exit Planning Advisor connected so well with my financial planning and wealth management practice; I don't know how a wealth manager could properly serve business owners without this background.

Are there common misconceptions about exit planning?

Kyle Bochat: Business owners think selling their business is much easier than it is. Unfortunately, the stats on exiting a business are pretty dim. According to a study conducted by the Exit Planning Institute, only one in three businesses that go on the market actually sell. So it's more complicated than people tend to believe.

Secondly, many business owners have a valuation in mind, often given to them at a cocktail party on the back of a napkin by someone within their industry whom they respect but who has not done a proper valuation of their entity. They may be entirely off base with what their business is worth. This often leads to falsely overvaluing the business or even undershooting in some situations. It is easy to base the value off of the sale of a peer company and assume that is what you will get when you exit, but there is the sales price, and then there are the terms of the deal. How much you net after taxes, the maturity and transition ability of your business, the risk you are willing to carry post-transaction, and the transition timeline are all details that must be factored in. No two deals are equal.

The term "exit planning" may imply that you can put it off until the end of your business lifecycle. Can you shed some light on this?

Kyle Bochat: The best exits are planned three to five years before you actually want to hang up your hat. And when I say "exits," it's a broad term. It is not necessarily a sale. It could be intergenerational or some handoff within your organization. But whatever the case, you cannot just raise your hand and say, "I'm ready to get out today." It's not that easy. Owners who wait too long to sell run the risk of becoming disengaged in the business, being forced out due to poor health, or having key personnel leave. These issues can detract from the value and salability of the business.

Are there pitfalls that can sabotage a successful exit?

Kyle Bochat: One of the biggest detriments to the sale of an enterprise is a business built on the back of the owner that is still reliant on the owner today. Owner-centric businesses cannot transition unless the owner plans to transition with the business. If you *are* the business, there is no business when you leave. That's why proper planning is necessary to ensure your team can carry on the work you've done so well over the years.

Can you give us a 10,000-foot view of what it looks like to work with you?

Kyle Bochat: I received my certification through the Exit Planning Institute. We have three gates we walk clients through. It starts with the **Discover** gate through a process called a triggering event. That's where we do a SWOT analysis of the business. We measure the tangible and intangible capital of the business, use actual deals or comps to determine an approximate valuation at its current status today, and then determine the potential of its value if the owner decides to grow over the coming years.

Once we've done that initial work and know what the asset looks like, we can transition into gate number two, the **Prepare** gate. During this phase, we focus on protecting the investment the owner has already built and growing it further. Owners must protect their business from specific issues that are almost inevitable such as death, disability, divorce, or disagreements among partners or employees. With patience and time, we help the owner develop and execute a value acceleration plan so they can increase their chances of harvesting more value upon exit. At this stage, owners may be introduced to insurance experts, legal and tax counsel, and dedicated growth coaches to assist with execution.

And finally, the third stop is the **Decide** gate. When the business is at a point where it is ready to transition, and the business owner feels like it's time, we quarterback, getting them in touch with an appropriate sales agent. That may be a business broker, someone within the mergers and acquisitions industry, or a banker who will assist with internal buyout programs.

These three gates are essential; I walk with them the entire way through.

Kyle, what inspired you to get started in this field?

Kyle Bochat: In financial planning, when you build a financial plan, you have to list all of the client's assets. For business owners, the lion's share of the assets is their business entity. I've encountered too many entrepreneurs that failed to plan properly and were left with a wealth gap too big to cover. My passion is to leave fewer business owners stranded financially and equip them with the knowledge, resources, and tools necessary for a successful exit and financial life.

Is there anything else you would like to share with business owners?

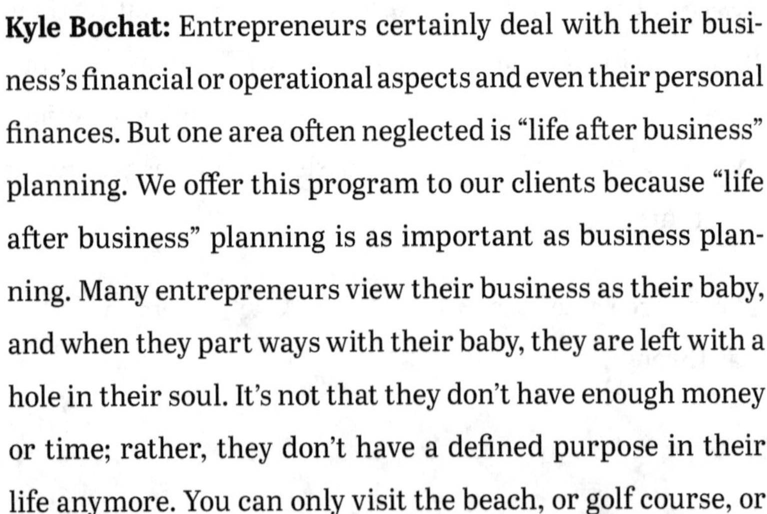

Kyle Bochat: Entrepreneurs certainly deal with their business's financial or operational aspects and even their personal finances. But one area often neglected is "life after business" planning. We offer this program to our clients because "life after business" planning is as important as business planning. Many entrepreneurs view their business as their baby, and when they part ways with their baby, they are left with a hole in their soul. It's not that they don't have enough money or time; rather, they don't have a defined purpose in their life anymore. You can only visit the beach, or golf course, or hike the mountains so much before it doesn't carry the same luster. Articulating what your next act will look like and what your mission and passion in life will be, is critical.

How can people find you, connect with you, and learn more?

Kyle Bochat: We do complimentary "get to know you sessions" to learn more about your business. You can set those up by phone at 770-534-0727 or email at kyle.bochat@lpl.com. Also, check us out online at www.sglwm.com.

Securities offered through LPL Financial, Member FINRA/SIPC. Advisory services offered through IFG Advisory, LLC, a registered investment advisor, SGL Wealth Management and IFG Advisory, LLC are separate entities from LPL Financial. ART#425771

KYLE BOCHAT,
CERTIFIED PRIVATE WEALTH ADVISOR®, CERTIFIED EXIT PLANNING ADVISOR®

SGL WEALTH MANAGEMENT

As Sr. Wealth Management Advisor at SGL Wealth Management, Kyle Bochat has had the privilege of helping many successful executives and business owners master their money so they can enjoy their life now AND increase their financial confidence. He's found that helping people plan first and then make investment decisions second leads to the results they are really after.

Over the course of Kyle's professional career, he's gained experience in diverse industries. Over the years, the skills acquired from careers in training and development, leadership, healthcare administration, and operating wealth management practices have added to his perspective on how to truly help entrepreneurs.

Kyle's private practice focuses exclusively on helping wealthy families and business owners grow, protect and transition their wealth. As a graduate of the Yale School of Management Private Wealth Advisor program and a Certified Exit Planning Advisor, he is experienced in navigating the complex challenges and opportunities common with having wealth and business assets.

In addition to wealth management and business exit consulting, Kyle is an experienced author having written the book, *M.A.X. Three Incredibly Simple Steps to Master Your Money.*

Kyle resides in NE, Georgia, with his wife Erin and three girls, Jaelynn, Natalie, and Mallory. He is an ASA-certified sailor, poor golfer, and active dad passionate about his faith, family, clients, and community.

EMAIL:

kyle.bochat@lpl.com

PHONE:

770-534-0727

WEBSITE:

sglwm.com

KYLE DANNER

KYLE DANNER

Conversation With Kyle Danner

Kyle, you are an exit planning advisor. Tell us about your work and the people you help.

Kyle Danner: I help business owners solve their number one challenge when running their company and, ultimately, their exit - their people. Using the Entrepreneurial Operating System, I work with the leadership team to improve **Vision**, **Traction**, and **Healthy**.

- **Vision:** Getting everyone on the same page with where they're going and a plan to get there.
- **Traction:** Instilling discipline and accountability so everyone executes the vision week in and week out.
- **Healthy:** Helping the leaders become a more open, functional, and cohesive team.

A healthy leadership team aligned with the company's vision using a proven process for execution allows the owner to build a business they can exit on their terms with maximum value.

A perfect example is a family business I coached where the parents wanted to pass the business off to their sons in five years. By implementing EOS, specifically the weekly scorecard that gave them transparency into the company's sales efforts, they completed the handoff in less than three.

How much thought do business owners put into exit planning?

Kyle Danner: This sounds harsh, but owners put little thought into exit planning. And that's understandable when you step into the owner's shoes. They know it's crucial to their family, finances, employees, and customers. But they're so busy running the business, solving issues, getting the work done, and taking care of their clients, that they don't take time to step out and work on the critical things like figuring out what drives the value of their organization.

Think of it this way. What feels more like a priority; landing a new customer that generates revenue or talking to your attorney about a buy/sell agreement or an insurance specialist about a key person policy? It's the tension between the urgent (running the business) and the important (working on the business).

Furthermore, there's more than one way to exit a business, each with a long list of considerations. So it's no wonder business owners put off exit planning.

Are there preconceived notions about exit planning?

Kyle Danner: A business owner often says, "I'm making a lot of money. I have a great lifestyle for my family; we're sending the kids to school and taking incredible vacations. So who wouldn't want to buy my company?" But they don't stop to think about taking themselves out of the day-to-day running of the business. They fail to see how hard it will be for someone else to step into their shoes and take over their company when all the systems and processes are in their head, and they're the keeper of the big relationships. They must understand that replacing themselves takes a lot of planning before they can even consider putting a "For Sale" sign on the business.

Are there pitfalls that can sabotage a successful sale?

Kyle Danner: The list of pitfalls that can sabotage a successful sale is long. The three I see most often are:

- Forgetting the value gap
- Starting too late
- Not developing their people

Let's take them one at a time:

- **Forgetting the value gap:** Owners start their exit planning with "How much is my business worth?" Instead, they must begin with, "How much will it cost to keep my lifestyle after I exit my company?" Usually, there's a gap between the two. The only way to fill that gap is to increase the value of the business so it sells at a higher multiple. That leads to the next pitfall.
- **Starting too late:** Preparing your company for sale takes tremendous work. So plan for at least three, potentially five years, to adequately prepare. But first, finding the right professional with experience selling your kind of company and who you trust takes time.

  Then, there's the work that follows once a valuation is completed. For example, you may find that your leadership team needs to improve in critical areas; processes must be documented or updated; your sales depend on one or two key customers not secured by contracts; your equipment requires updating or replacement, etc. That takes time and effort in addition to running the daily operations.

- **Not developing their people:** I sound like a broken record, but I must stress the importance of developing your leadership team, the next level of managers, and your workforce. Buyers don't want to purchase a problem. They want a turnkey operation. Next to sound financials, dependable and repeatable customers, and efficient, documented systems, they want a healthy culture with a strong leadership team in place.

  Owners overlook this because it's the most challenging aspect of exit planning. Typically, owners have a long-term, loyal workforce. However, that loyalty may not transfer to the new ownership. Or, the new owners have aggressive growth plans that the existing workforce needs to be more skilled to meet. If owners need to invest in their people, they're overwhelmed by the options. Do they need leadership, sales, or management training? Furthermore, how do they measure the ROI when investing in their people? Unlike buying a new piece of equipment to increase production capacity to sell more widgets, measuring the benefit of management training feels impossible.

Kyle, what inspired you to get started in this field?

Kyle Danner: My personal experience in exiting my family's business. I joined my family's company right out of college. I planned to stay for one year but stayed for 17. We grew it from about $2 million in revenue with a dozen employees to over $18 million and over 80 employees. We became the fifth-largest printing company in Kansas City and a recognized leader in the industry. And yes, I'm bragging because I'm proud of what we accomplished.

Of course, with that much growth, there was a lot of change. One was the family business and I were no longer a fit. Recognizing that, I made the difficult decision to leave everything I knew and strike out on my own. In my next chapter, I thought I wanted to be a therapist. Make whatever connection you want about a career in mental health after working in your family's business for 17 years!

However, I stumbled upon the field of family business advising and saw how you could keep the family and business healthy and whole. Reflecting on my experience, I realized I didn't exit well from my family's business because we didn't know how to navigate the business, financial, and emotional aspects. That set me on a path to working with over 25 family businesses and countless advisors to help the families prepare for the next chapter in the business.

Along the way, I earned the Certified Exit Planning Advisor (CEPA) designation from the Exit Planning Institute to deepen my understanding of value creation and exit planning.

Then, my world changed when someone handed me the book *Traction: Get a Grip on Your Business* by Gino Wickman. I saw how a proven process with simple, practical tools could profoundly impact the families and companies I work with. I became a Professional EOS Implementer and now spend my days helping leadership teams get everything they want from their business.

Is there anything else you would like to share with business owners?

Kyle Danner: Business owners fear addressing the subject with their leadership team because they're worried about creating drama and key people possibly leaving. However, if you're in your 50s or 60s, your leadership team and everybody else in the company is already thinking about it.

Since it's on everyone's mind, start talking about it with your team so they can help you prepare well. Remember, it's in their best interest to build a healthy, sustainable company that will continue to provide good jobs for your employees and positively impact your community. Think of it as establishing a legacy that will last as you enter the next chapter of your life.

How can people find you, connect with you, and learn more?

Kyle Danner: Email me at kyle.danner@eosworldwide.com. I'll give you and your leadership team 90 minutes of my time and show you how EOS can transform your business.

KYLE DANNER

PROFESSIONAL EOS IMPLEMENTER®
EOS WORLDWIDE

Kyle Danner began his entrepreneurial career in his family's printing company, where he became an owner and helped the firm grow from $2 million to $18+ million in revenue. He then made the difficult decision to leave it all behind. His passion for helping people led to a degree in counseling, and his love for family business inspired him to help 30+ families and their advisors grow, transition, or exit their businesses.

Since then, he has expanded his focus beyond family business to working with organizations of all sizes and stages of growth. Along the way, he discovered that business owners and their leadership teams need a simple, practical way to run their companies. That's why he became a Professional EOS Implementer®. EOS®, the Entrepreneurial Operating System®, provides a structure and process to help business owners and their leadership teams clarify, simplify, and achieve their vision for the business.

EMAIL:
kyle.danner@eosworldwide.com

PHONE:
913.481.5909

WEBSITE:
eosworldwide.com/kyle-danner

LINKEDIN:
linkedin.com/in/kyleldanner/

RIK SAYLOR

RIK SAYLOR

CONVERSATION WITH RIK SAYLOR

Rik, you are a certified exit planning advisor. Tell us about your work and the people you help.

Rik Saylor: I work primarily with Main Street to middle-market businesses. I have loved small businesses for almost my entire life. I started with a paper route, had my first company when I was 20, and was in the financial industry by 23, and it's grown from there. Wealth management has been my lifelong endeavor, solving challenges for individuals and business owners. I've been in the industry for 43 years and have had my own company for 27.

Business owners are hardworking, intelligent people who don't have much time to work on their business when they are working in it. It's heartbreaking to know that eight out of ten businesses will die, they'll never transition to the next level or the next generation, and somebody's life's work is gone. In the financial industry, that statistic is even worse. The attrition rate is nine out of ten.

It comes down to the fact that people don't plan to fail; they fail to plan. They're too busy in their day-to-day life. And I will separate lifestyle businesses from enterprise businesses because the lifestyle business *is* the owner. So when they die, there isn't anything to pass on other than assets. But on the other side, there's equity, recurring revenue, and multiples. I come across all kinds of business owners, and I haven't found one who doesn't want to be good. But the ones who I ideally work with are the ones who want to be great.

As a CEPA, I adhere to the discipline of 5-4-3-2-1. There are five stages of maturity in any business: I-dentify, P-rotect, B-uild, H-arvest, and M-anage. The goal is to increase value and decrease risks.

There are four intangible capitals: Human, Social, Customer, and Structural:

HUMANS are who run companies, and having the "right people in the right seats, rowing in the same direction" is imperative.

SOCIAL is the culture and chemistry of any team. Teams that flow together grow together and win continuously.

CUSTOMERS are the heartbeat of every business. The "right ones" and duplicating those that fit your core values are priceless. They do more business with you, refer more customers like themselves, and provide a win-win scenario.

STRUCTURAL encompasses everything that makes your company flow efficiently. Processes, documentation, training, technology, tools, equipment, and real estate all fit into this category of most regarded intangibles/tangible assets.

There are three gaps: Wealth, Profit, and Value. The Wealth gap is the difference between where you are now and where your ideal life goals and dreams are.

The Profit gap represents the possible shortfall of your company not being all it can be. This is more than a slogan; this is real money lost due to not being "best-in-class" in your particular industry.

The Value gap is the profit gap number vs. the potential sale price as of today compared to the top multiple companies in your industry. Simply stated, it pays in spades to be "best-in-class."

If you don't address the business, financial, and personal aspects, like any three-legged stool, it would be a non-starter. Although these are closely related, they are distinctly individual. Without any one of these not properly addressed, you'll have firewood because there aren't one or two-legged stools. Particularly, personal planning stands out because it's often the most overlooked and needs to be explored. Don't forget to ask the key questions and discuss them with your spouse/significant other, for sanity's sake! That could be why a recent survey revealed that of the 1 out of 5 businesses that do sell, 73% of the owners deeply regretted having sold their life's work. While you may think it would be price, it was likely because they sold their purpose for being.

I like to refer to this as Y-2. The most important aspects are the year you were born, the year you find out why you are here, and what you accomplish between the "dash." The gifts we are born with, and everyone has, are our gifts from God. What we do with them is our gift back to Him and our fellow man.

Two concurrent paths must be addressed in any business owner's journey. Business and personal have a considerable impact on our lives. Also referred to as the work/life balance, we can have our ideal life as we fulfill our purpose on earth. What does it profit a person if they have all the financial success in life but lose their health, family, or joy of life? Exiting your business at age 60 or 70, you can expect another 20 to 30 years of lifespan. Staying healthy can help make that healthspan when the quality of life meets quantity.

I know that business owners put in long hours, even on their vacations. Consider that a business that is owner dependent is also valued less and may not be transferable. Working ON your business while working IN your business is one of the, if not THE, biggest challenges that most owners face. Great news! You can simultaneously build revenue stream and enterprise value when the right people, processes, performance indicators, and property utilization are clear and accountable.

Last but not least is that every business owner will exit their business. The key questions are: 1- How ATTRACTIVE is your business in the eyes of a potential buyer? and 2- How READY are you/your business for this inevitable event? These are scalable by comparing your company to your industry and competitors. Another way of asking this is: How significant is your company? Do you want to be the best you/your company can be? What's your legacy?

Are there preconceived notions about exit planning that prevent successful exits?

Rik Saylor: In my business, I'd like to say I learned a lot from my mistakes. And I'd like other people to learn from my mistakes. I should have focused on KPIs (Key Performance Indicators). The difference between running a good business and a great business breaks into four key areas: Maximizing profitability, operations, sales, and continuity strategies. There is no difference between a company that is just well run and one that's ready to exit or what I like to call "built to sell."

It's essential to focus on the continuity plan, the dress rehearsal for the real thing. What will happen when something unexpected happens in the form of one of the 5 Ds (death, divorce, disability, disagreement, or disaster)? Every business owner will exit someday, whether you exit with the biggest chest full of money because you planned, looked at the tax strategies, explored the different avenues, considered various buyers, and did all your work, or you're going to go out in a casket or on a gurney. Everyone is going to exit, and everybody has a plan. But you don't want the default one.

Many hardworking, smart business owners have built good companies, yet being a great one is elusive. Focusing ON the business while IN the business with an objective viewpoint is priceless. This is where a professional team of advisors is worth their weight in gold!

When is the right time to start exit planning?

Rik Saylor: Somebody could sell their business within six months. I'd like to compare this to selling a house. My father was in real estate for 37 years, and he loved the business, and I've got friends who do that. Even though selling a business is not like selling a house, that's how most owners approach it. They think, "Hey, you know what? I will sell it in five years. And I'll do that five years from now." But they need to realize that the five-year mark is the red zone. For example, the red zone is at the 20-yard line in football. Great teams score touchdowns, good teams score something, and great teams also win championships. If you want to optimize your business and the margin of error is minimal, you need three years at the very least to prepare your business for an exit.

It took me three years to work on the business in my own company. And I'm trained in it. It involves bringing a lot of professionals in and getting things in line. Three years is the minimum, five years is excellent, and ten years is not too soon. I think of it like a ship on the horizon. You look at the horizon; the farther you are out, you can make some mistakes and adjustments and still get there. But when you get close, this is where ships collide. Ask anyone on the Titanic. That didn't work out too well.

"Begin with the end in mind" is one of my favorite focus points for this discussion. Work your way back to now and determine what needs to be done, how, when, and by who. This simple exercise will uniquely provide the answer for the "right time" for every business owner.

Rik, what inspired you to get started in this field?

Rik Saylor: Every great professional has a coach. If you don't have one, I implore you to get one. I've had a business coach for about six years, and I wish I had done it earlier in my career. I'm a good golfer, but I'm not great. But I love it. And I've improved because I put more time in and started playing with better people because I learned from them. One of my best investments was hiring a golf pro to videotape, analyze and instruct me on my golf swing. He was like the Bagger Vance of golf instructors and asked when I began playing golf. My response was the previous 18 years, to which he responded,

"No, you just started now when you got serious about it!" So having somebody sit outside your business and give you that same coaching is essential.

My passion for helping people achieve their potential came from my family/faith. My father and mother possessed and passed on values of hard work, love, honesty, gratitude, and treating others with respect. There were three times in my life when I thought I might be a minister. I redirected my talents when I experienced multiple reactions from others when they suddenly became disingenuous when I was perceived as a "man of the cloth."

I'm reminded of a parable about the three workers and talents (which has a double meaning of a currency and attributes). An owner gave the same amount of "seed money" to each of them before going away. Upon his return, he visited each of them to see what they had accomplished in his absence. The first worker responded by returning the original money stating that he knew his boss to be very conservative and didn't want to risk any of his hard-earned cash. The second one gave back the original and a bit more saying he wanted to give back more than he had received. The remaining employee had multiplied the original amount by four times! The owner then took from the other two and gave it to the wise and faithful one.

I saw then and there that my path would maximize my God-given "talents" by helping others achieve their goal of financial independence because while the love of money/power may be the "root of all evil," the lack of it severely hampers a lot of good that can be accomplished. Money is simply a means to an end and the best avenue of barter.

Business owners are smart people, and the middle class is the backbone of America. But they don't have time to work in and on the business. They get to the end of that 40 or 60-hour week, and no energy is left. So it's great to have somebody to coach, analyze, and say, "Hey, let's just copy success. We don't have to reinvent the wheel here. Let's go find what great companies look like."

I'm trained in that. And my passion is to help business owners implement different systems just like I did. And again, I love it. I love coming to work. People always ask me about the wealth management side, "When are you going to retire?" When it's not fun anymore, or I don't have a passion for it. Or I find something I like more. But this is a fantastic part of my life. I'm passionate about what I do and who I do it for.

Is there anything else you would like to share with business owners?

Rik Saylor: People constantly wonder where to begin. It can be overwhelming when you open up the hood of your business, look at the engine, and find out what is not running well. But our job is to ensure it is hitting on all cylinders at peak efficiency to hit the top marks. The reward is having a better-valued company and higher revenue, which improves your life.

Maximizing profitability, optimizing operations, maximizing sales, and continuity strategies are the four cornerstones to building, growing, and preparing your company to become the very best it can be. Balance working on/in your work week, and don't fear not knowing how to get to your ideal life. Invest the time necessary by blocking out your calendar to add one more idea than you knew before and implement it. I love sharing what so many successful great leaders execute regularly and consistently.

The best way to start is to get a valuation to create a baseline and determine your company's current position. We offer a very inexpensive valuation for under $3,000, while the national average is $8,000. We can professionally analyze your business, answer your questions, and help you develop a solid starting point.

Next, build your battle box. What happens when the proverbial "stuff" hits the fan and a pandemic hits? If you are in crisis mode, who do you contact? Will you open your doors the next day? Or will all of your clients, customers, and employees disappear?

Those are the top two items to begin planning your exit. Getting the right professionals to help you achieve these tasks is key to success.

How can people find you, connect with you, and learn more?

Rik Saylor: First, you must misspell Red correctly. It's REDDE, and my website is www.REDDE-ZONE.com. On the homepage, anyone may download my FREE e-book, "Exit Smart," and sign up for a complimentary subscription to the "Redde-Zone Exit Insights" e-newsletter. Look for my weekly podcast/minutes, "Redde-Zone Business Tips," where I interview great company owners so that you can copy their successes and avoid their mistakes! In addition, if you're READY, you can select "Get a Valuation." It will take you to our landing page, where you are welcome to engage us and start a conversation.

RIK SAYLOR

CERTIFIED EXIT PLANNING ADVISOR/
WEALTH MANAGER
REDDE-ZONE BUSINESS CONSULTING

As President and Practitioner, Rik started RSF in 1996 and has advised hundreds of families and business owners to grow, use, and pass wealth on to loved ones. Rik's development of an independent client best interest firm allows them the liberty of providing holistic, financially objective advice to the families and businesses they serve. Taking the time to listen and learn about each client's unique situation is essential. As an Investment Advisory Representative, Rik offers truly comprehensive financial planning with an awareness of lifestyle and income needs. His "team" approach, by planning collaboratively with CPAs, insurance agents, and attorneys, assists in navigating a competent, successful financial future.

As a Fairfield Chamber of Commerce member, Rik was selected and honored as the Business Person of the Year in 2010. Rik is an avid reader and has a curiosity and hunger for learning. Rik wrote/taught curriculum as a volunteer instructor for the OLLI program (Osher Lifelong Learning Institute) for five years at the University of Cincinnati and the University of Dayton. Past host of "Straight Talk-Clear Decisions," Rik shared financial insights weekly with listeners on the internet and radio, enlightening them to make better financial decisions.

Since 2002 Rik and Kim have been a blended family of five children and three grandchildren so far. Rik loves the outdoors, whether golfing, biking, motorcycling, or boating. At their lake house, Rik relaxes and listens to music or reads a book when he's not working on a project or hanging out with neighbors. He loves having his family and friends out to the lake house whenever possible, as they love to host concerts, parties, and fun. When it comes to life, Rik loves to win but, most importantly, must compete for the fun of it.

EMAIL:

rik@redde-zone.com

PHONE:

513-454-1360

WEBSITE:

redde-zone.com

OTHER:

BESTOFBIZSOLUTIONS.com

ABOUT THE PUBLISHER

Mark Imperial is a Best-Selling Author, Syndicated Business Columnist, Syndicated Radio Host, and internationally recognized Stage, Screen, and Radio Host of numerous business shows spotlighting leading experts, entrepreneurs, and business celebrities.

His passion is to discover noteworthy business owners, professionals, experts, and leaders who do great work and share their stories and secrets to their success with the world on his syndicated radio program titled "Remarkable Radio."

Mark is also the media marketing strategist and voice for some of the world's most famous brands. You can hear his voice over the airwaves weekly on Chicago radio and worldwide on iHeartRadio.

Mark is a Karate black belt; teaches Muay Thai and Kickboxing; loves Thai food, House Music, and his favorite TV shows are infomercials.

Learn more:

www.MarkImperial.com
www.BooksGrowBusiness.com

www.ingramcontent.com/pod-product-compliance
Lightning Source LLC
LaVergne TN
LVHW020047110826
845155LV00029B/662

* 9 7 8 1 9 5 4 7 5 7 3 4 9 *